What the Psychic Said
By Grace Cavalieri

WHAT THE PSYCHIC SAID
By Grace Cavalieri

First Edition

Library of Congress cataloguing in publication:
2019921059

Published in the United States by GOSS183
Copyright ®2020 Grace Cavalieri

ISBN 13: 978-1-5136-5706-6

Publisher: GOSS183
Cover photo: "Bar Harbor" by Dan Murano, from the book *Poet Trees*
Book Design: April Carter Grant

www.gracecavalieri.com
www.poetsandartists.com
www.goss183.com

What the Psychic Said

Dedicated to my children,
grandchildren and great-grandson

Grateful Acknowledgments

Ovunquesiamo1 "Just this," "Help Me Here," "Making Meaning"

About Place Journal "Athena's Little Secret," "You ask Me About Resistance"

SoFloPoJo "Tony Hoagland Is Dead," "The Mazurka," "The Sound Haunting Makes," "Harbinger"

Poetry Bay "Dirt"

Fearless Anthology "Come To a Wedding"

Lips "Quelly Looks Up From The Ground," "This Poem Is Asking For Your Love"

The Bhubanes Review "The Octopus Poems"

Wildword "The Picnic By The Ocean"

Italian Americana "May Day"

PLUME "Weather Report," "Letter from Puerto Rico," "Once upon A Hummingbird"

Lummox "Prophecy," "Refugees," "Athena Tells the Truth"

PoetsArtists "The Hunk," "What the Psychic Said," "Hollow," "White," "Athena," "Telecommunications," "In Praise of The Oasis"

Loch Raven Review "I Have Come Down for Time to Tell You"

Innisfree Journal "Dancing in The Dark"

King's Estate Anthology "Help Me Here"

Delaware Poetry Review "The Prince and the Pauper," "Poppies in The Sky"

CONTENTS

Poem in dialogue with Dan Murano's cover photo, "Bar Harbor"
Credit: *Poet Trees*, 2019

GUARDIAN OF TIME

I don't know how I knew this –
This deepening love – subjectivity of experience –
The desolation of the prairie rabbit –
How the sky and the air can turn pink
For no reason.
We would not have seen the pink
Unless there were sun beaming down, its
Wishes closing in, guarding our treasures,
Answering the question:
How to love without fear
Just look at the ball of sun behind the tree
Now a deepening orange
Now a fanning behind the branches
Like images in God's dream—
Did you think there was an easier access to happiness?

--Grace Cavalieri

The Octopus Poems

THE PICNIC BY THE OCEAN

The Octopus offers me one of his three hearts,
briar and holly for friendship in the second and third,
saved for times of longing, times of loss.
A strange romance, I admit –
Friends would never approve or believe,
yet he was untouched by human hands.
How can we say this is not a source of wonder—
"Who will sing my song, if not you?" he asked.
"Who will dream of me, as I lay under the stillness of water?"
Even an Octopus can be eloquent, and then again,
as we know, enormous need can become power.
What am I supposed to do now?
I stand by the water,
my woolen dress unraveling in the waves.

THE OCTOPUS HAS THREE HEARTS

With seaweed in my hair, I enter.
Sun skims on top of the blue as I become one with my breath,
my lover sinks, flies down beyond currents.
it's not unpleasant
until now I realize how each shell is without birdsong.
Shadows loom, waving yellow to amber then blue,
colors never seen before,
--you just have to go deep enough--
pieces of wreckage, pieces of what may have been flesh.
What have I given up to get something I did not want?
I never desired the octopus,
I just didn't want anyone else to have him.
Is that wrong? Or just human? And who am I,
right now, swimming like a fish,
--to speak of being human--
a traitor to all air and sunflower. I gave up feet in
warm sand, my bonnet, a chair, cycles of stars, for a
promise, and what was that secret now? I forget.
Is to marry a sea creature a sin? And what is sex below the surface?
Just when I think he's gone he appears: : ubiquitous: :autonomous: :
filling all space – he'll never leave me alone – he says.
That's what worries me, I think.
It must be evening – I see clouds inciting the water,
water reserved now for the last dark.
He wraps his arms around me and holds on.

MY OCTOPUS

I don't mind if I'm not his kind.
I get along with everyone, using pleasantries
from other times for passersby – *have a good day*
do you think it will snow. Is it warm
enough for you?
Everyone likes me even if I have only one heart.
I look everywhere for him, through fog on water –
while a large grey mammal with one eye
never leaves me, he's a good companion,
although an unlikely friend, we get along.
The sky lowers, making my loneliness exorbitant—
I'd never leave my octopus unloved
for I wouldn't wish this for an octopus or
anything like an octopus.
For one moment fleeting I thought I saw him behind the coral
pink satiny rocks shimmers of green,
a strike of light, blue enough to make me happy while I wait.
My grey creature moves closer than I'd like, whispering
This is not your world what did you expect when you follow an octopus?
There's a cold front coming. I see a scuttling under rocks. A fear.
Grey creature moves even closer. In the distance I see waves of light
pink waves pink light moving ripples of water.
He's coming for me. My beloved. He's coming for me.

RED IS NOT THE COLOR OF MY HEART

No one wants me to stay with my octopus
The psychiatrist says I'm too dependent –
that's why my octopus swims far away every day.
My healer says it opens me up
to all kinds of underworld disruptions.
My doctor says I'm not eating right:
prawns, worms, mollusks, fish –
This is when I float to the top
listening to my heart bubbling
in every direction,
spinning and sailing until
it breaks on rock.
The gray mammal says stay true to yourself.
I have no self. I gave it to the octopus,
he takes care of me.
Once when asked to touch his eight tentacles
I swam away, I thought he said testicles.
That's why I cannot have children,
my fear.
No one believes I can love an octopus
Why spend your time? They say.
Why? because he has only three years to live,
This is why my heart is green

MURAL

You'd look at him, and say, "He's just an octopus" – slippery skin,
                    barnacles, suction for touch,"
But have you tried to turn away from someone who reclaims
not with manace but with love
and adoration? I know
I'm not as graceful as my creature
and I adapt slowly – I plant flowers,
that do not grow – I make a house that floats away – I sing and
                    choke on songs
without breath – the ground keeps changing beneath my feet,
that's what marriage is here they say,
And that is what's between us. What? A wilderness of water we
                    try to cross.
That's why we stay. For this pursuit.
I miss my own tears, not part of his brine – the multiply into foam—
No one cries here   No one laughs
Some days we go where
a child brings childhood joy back to joy – I think I'm growing tired
                    of the color blue.

WHAT TO KEEP

I'm lost again within the thin skin of time,
My Octopus pretends he never loved me—
Wait, When, I ask "When?"
After he stopped needing me, he said.
Beneath the mask, one tear escapes his dying eye,
becomes the water's surface, where I, rising
look around—the glaring noise,
the sounds, buses, and rocket ships,
This could never happen under.
Clouds form animals in the sky,
how they dissolve beneath me—
Nowhere to go but deeper
to where I feel most at home,
to the last light surrounding my shoulders
into the glass of sea, cold and wet with first waves,
I go alone toward open currents
toward the family of pale shadows beckoning me—
Did you know that Squid live forever?
It's a fact and
my beautiful Squid wants me. He may vanquish me
but he will never die.

SEA BELT

Do you know what it is to
          dive   leave the
coast line
          move through the silky suds
rugged reefs
while above you
               the goldfinch
sweeps down
          catching midair
a beautiful description
of your past world
I'm here now. That's all
that matters
I stood on the shore
wondering what was beneath
blue hoods of waves I stood
looking upward and out
          at
the land
not knowing what could be felt
    the unrise of
          swimming on the back of
milky foam just above
rusting read ship wrecks
I want to stop losing the past with its grind of dust
and dirt with its cuds
               of lost dry grasses
I want to raise
          the net of memory
filled with wiggling silver
slippery fish
where the starving eat the decayed
washed clean.

STALKED

1.

HOW IT STARTED

The muscular man invited her
for dinner.

Unused to romance,
she invited her husband along.

Oh these were the days,
so innocent

she filled her living room
with water to take a swim,

after the frolic her new friend
held her underwater.

This is not right, she spoke, but
the words floated and no one heard.

2.

THE STALKER

She saw Don Juan again taking out
the garbage,

her face still swollen from
pulling off the bandage.

This is why he sent her chapstick,
And tic tacs, orange and white.

The water of discontent
kept her away from her thirst.

If this is the only self you have
would you really give it to him?

She felt when someone hugged her
they didn't really mean it.

but he said *he* did and I think she came
to feel that nothing could destroy her.

The party was for young people
but there was that stranger again.

He ran his fingers under each half
of her breasts as if she wouldn't notice.

When he pretended she wasn't there
she tried to act young, although she was not.

3.

WANTING LESS

When needs go wrong
she needed less
until she didn't need anything at all.

The crab in the nets
let go
trusting the dark
the way they do,

dropping in like they do,
when they let go.

She thought she could
master it by inviting him to lunch,

get rid of him that way.

After 50 more phone calls
he talked her into dinner.

4.

ANCIENT RITES AND MODERN DESIRES

When she was young
she always wanted
someone there waiting for her

but not this.

I make no concessions he said and
she wanted him to open a concession stand
to grant her some.

She looks for help – for race
creed or national origin.

The street is bare and
no one is there
but a hidden corner that's not safe.

He jumps out from a bush
grabbing her arm
saying

*When you find something
are you allowed to keep it?*

5.

THIS IS HOW SHE IMAGINED GETTING AWAY

Although
the bank
was covered
with snow
she owned
no coat
she scrambled
up without
slipping
she was not cold.

6.

THE ESCAPE

Leaving the bungalow
with its melancholy rooms
she was running from
everything she saw
even the geese on the porch,
the fat lady watering her lawn.

She ran toward the gray sign
with white paint
saying   THIS WAY

Passing the nursing home
the twittering old ladies sat
dressing up their years of marriage
with dreams of someone coming home.

There they are in clean dresses
hair combed, talcum on the neck
talking like grown people while
becoming little girls again.

Looking for help down route 17
not much had changed
not even the broken duck
with a wound in its side,
still loping up rocks
trying to keep up.

Try as she did
she couldn't get the strong ones
away from him
no matter how much
cracked corn she imagined.

7.

TELECOMMUNICATION

She wore a golden whistle
Around her neck
Like a cross
Which caught
The light
Whenever she walked.

8.

THE END

Before the sun came up
Nature was already
Greeting a new day
With thanks for
Tender mercies.

He left like a
Squirrel twisting
His body
To make a hole
And she let it all go
Keeping only in hand what
A person can do.

9.

GOING BACK TO WORK

In a dress with pink around
the hem

a dress she put on backwards

wearing shoes
with no tops

without a sweater

spilling mud splashed on papers
leaving the house in the dark

not even a light in her office
dirty walls in the room

she was so weak

her dead mother
had to come back
to make the children their lunch.

10.

WRONG THINGS

She tried to keep the house
        from floating away
            bought heavy furniture
    carried in the couch.

She thought she could
        hold anything to get it
            from one place to another.

This is why she was covered
        with bruises
            and lifted anyway.

She is so slim. She wears a long silken dress.
        She handed me a poem, her first,
            framed in Italian Byzantine.

It read surprisingly well. The last line
        said,

He finally had me,
my cheeks pricked by tears

I didn't know whether to
        take up the word *pricked*
                it was her first poem after-
                        all.

The blood from the swelling
        on her right forearm dripped
                in the shape of a tear

wet with her first speech.

        This is progress I thought
                her finally speaking.

The beautiful must be as vulnerable
        as anyone else
                for when I ask why she

accepted his flowers
        she said
                I wanted to feel alive.

11.

BROKEN AND ENTERED

When in her sleep
    she held her arms
        straight out and pointed

they said, never keep a gun
    in a house with a
        sleepwalker and

he was let go.

She was guilty as charged
    carrying terror
        without a license.

The fluids of self-doubt
    on the bathroom floor
        were stained white.

When the man in a mask entered
        her, she filed claims.
They took her to headquarters
    and gave her some drugs.

POEMS
AND
MEDITATIONS

DIRT

The neighbors are trying to catch them,
the fat red fox with a fluffy tail,
and the lean mean gray scraggly one,
shitting on our pavement,
daring to walk the lawn,
his tail is long and sharp as a rat's,
he has patches of mange all over,
his eyes glitter as we pull children inside,
he dares us with his hunger,
his disease, his decided defiance,
the neighbors will win, they'll get him,
he's getting weaker
but still he runs.
A blonde triathlete calls out, runs by to say,
hey look at that red fox how fat
I wonder what he's eating
keep your cats inside.

While "Red," proud and dapper, illumined by the sun,
— the healthy one— dances,
dances on our chrysanthemums,
he has no grief,
he's mindless, but partial to mice and,
comes from thousands of nomadic animals,
survived magically from forest,
to our neat cul-de-sac. I'm attracted to the sick one,
and want to leave him food but,
the apples out back go to the deer.
I don't know how he survives, homeless,
in fields of hunger, poverty, cold, sickness.
Once when I was young across the back yard,
lived Laura Doll, she was tall, thin as a pencil,
with straight stringy red hair,
her father was a conductor,
on the railroad track three doors away,
She would wave to him each day,
I envied their relationship.
Once she told me that every night,
she took off her dirty underwear,
and folded it neatly in her drawer for the next day,
once I thought that was the worst thing in the world
that could ever happen.

THE MAZURKA

From the Marsh of human discontent,
from the grave of self-doubt,
came a spark of life, a long distance
phone call from
four young Rappers who
knew how I'd been
grieving from lack of fame.
They offered
me a Residency in
South America and they
spoke of my breaking the
mold with my work
in libraries.
They said I'd make quite
a splash on YouTube, but
when I asked if it was
because of my elevated
language, they said,
to be honest, it's because,
when you danced
your nipples showed through.
My husband said he'd come with me
and was proud
of my recognition
among literary historians.

HARBINGER

You'll never get it finished
Don't even try
You can never return a life payment of kindness and hurt
You'll never arouse
          your first love again
You'll never learn the geography
Of the archipelago or name
Those yellow flowers shaped like angels by the side of the road
And you don't even care anymore
About who bought you the white straw hat
You'll never visit the snow in Russia
Or play chess
Or service a computer
Forget it
Not in this lifetime
Your skin will never be soft and pink as your first child's
Nothing is left
So just be good
Don't try to be good.
BE Good. How? Don't ask
Just do it
The rest is none of your business.

DANCING IN THE DARK

The party is in full swing
And I was the only one who could see you

although I thought you should be apparent
to all our dearest guests.

The day drifted like a cold picture –
Our futures filled with someone else's blood.

In the forest of skeletons
one perfect day, I thought.

Then I made the mistake
just as the wind sometimes does

of asking the guests what color shirt you were wearing,
so bright and awake, it seemed you were visible.

Everyone was puzzled and made guesses –
I thought they saw you singing out colors.

Only I knew. I was the only one.
It was blue. It was blue.

THE SOUND THAT HAUNTING MAKES

I'd like to talk about how the day went, talk as we used to do,
not with singing words, but smaller celebrations gathered until
we noticed the ridges of each other –
the missing parts that no one else could see.

I don't mind that you're away, an understandable
shift – aerodynamic in fact – you loved to fly – but
that you would forget me is impossible.
Did you see this sweater's lost a button loop?

And that excessive fruit makes the basket spill?
Are you laughing at my decorating skill?
Are you assuring me the problem is in the straw,
it's weaving, the oversized pear, the lopsided chair?

I'd like some decisions from you, yet I understand –
as a passenger of time – you are beyond my reach.
I need some help with perceptions, logistics –
teaching myself to live under the weight of visibility.

Since we seem to be of two different geographic climes,
can you direct me closer to you? You, who flew from Japan
to California using only the stars. Should I sit here in the sun
or move my hands, my heart, a little to the left?

I understand these are contradictory criteria –
the living and the dead – yet at times, through my devotion
to the past, plus my unreasonable emotions, I feel a
radiant warmth encircling me. Of course, at other times
the cumulative effect of memory left on its own is staggering.
Yesterday, you were solid as stone, rich with detail, revolving around me,
and other days like this one, I'm sure you understand,
It's as if it never happened.

TONY HOAGLAND IS DEAD
> *Grief is the medicine in her mouth*

Birds caught in my heart
All night the birds taped inside
Let them go
Pressed against the pane
Beyond the wisteria
Tony is dead
All the equations in the world
Are blank
Birds, you can be Maria's laugh in the kitchen
Birds, you can be New Hampshire
Fly, run, leap, row, Birds, while you can.

LEASH

The little girl in the white gown never cries
although she's shy when left with the lady
at the boarding house who is neither
nice nor mean
she stretches her arms goodbye knowing her destiny
she plays with the other children
and eats their food
while dwelling between this life
and waves of remembrance
why was she left there a month before needed
an extra time to get her used to strange surroundings
it's house
that was the month that started her walking
that extra month
that is what made her gown blow in the wind
staying outside in the dark
roaming the fields for an answer
three months was the bargain but four
a tragic tree she must look for and
find even if there is good reason for distance without joy –
does that mean it never happened? And did it? Happen?

PATTERN

Woman in the tree,
look upward away from
your frozen past.
Each branch is richly
poured with snow,
yet the limbs wasted
of earth are made of mist,
a feast that will rise
and melt toward the yellow
sun. Until then love what
you can. Once estranged
from yourself, captive as
winter's vixen, you were alone in
your heart's forest, watching
the day turned away from itself.
You might remember, if you try,
the surprise when you opened
your eyes to see in the coming
dark behind the snowcloud
a starry burst waiting to be seen.

ONCE UPON A HUMMINGBIRD

Soon we thought we
Knew everyone we needed to know
The glistening berries on a card
The new lawn, its quiet

After we walked on the
Confetti of crape Myrtle
There was nothing we couldn't trespass

Far from sleep came
A return from the distance
Where someone is dying

Tiny breezes, waiting trees
Petals released

Now before autumn
A red cup for the smallest of birds
Before migration across eternity

For this hour I wondered
What Forever looked like
Now I know it's an epiphany
Above the door sipping sugar water

Whirring with silence.

THE TEST OF SUNLIGHT

Athena said love was not what
        she hoped it would be
it was fractious and better
a vital moment in time scattered
        it was an "I have to go" hymn
the circle where everything else
was outside and without it
        so many pages to fill
the stare of remembrance
how do I understand this
        believe me it appears
arbitrary the law that governs
        is a fresh start
it's the significance of sorrow
        facts and theories
held in the heart
    oh sure trade secrets
and social change assembled
on the path
        a rich role in society
a grandeur reconciled
        legitimacy then why it is that
Athena is only alive even with love
when living through words

I'VE COME DOWN FROM TIME TO LET YOU KNOW

that summer was a great experiment
Before the approaching dryness of autumn

The children have taken off their boots
Their glasses are empty
We heard the distant sound of their leaving
What we feared most, the rain
The blue sky taken by it
The idle Hill where
Nothing is living on its earth

Once all their hands were sticky with blueberries
This taken from us and then
As if made of air, he, my husband
Too – changed from words to light

Once a man and a woman together
Remember me for that

Our lives happened there
In no special place
No special house
But the street turned blue
At midnight everywhere we went

And we owned what little
There was like a wing moving
But still ours

Just as if intended
Everything changed
The land grew red as clay
And the strong clear focus
Of the sun left its yellow singing

Do you understand that there was much to thank
Everything was common and true
Even the dish and the stairs
As if nothing existed before

Beauty wanted us and
Sometimes we failed
But there was at least
The window
The clouds – we'd say
Look at that sunflower
How full, how tall

My right hand across the table
Holding his left
Every square on the cloth
A flower

I'm not saying it was always seeing
Green leaves, large like on Maple trees
Yet there were moments that opened
One time a picnic on the sand.

DREAM, THIS TIME, NOT DEATH THAT TOOK HIM

but a woman.
Molecules of intensity, the curve of her arm,
the exchange –

How far does this map extend
measuring what voyage?
Night's cerebral link knows false

thought can make up
mosaics of betrayal
(But what if dreams tell the truth?)

I sleep in a stone gown on a flat marble bed –
What part of me would compose such a story

without death's gentle logic?
Even this, I want to share with him.
Reluctant as I am for another day

a finely balanced cardinal feeds on his bin,
vibrant, red, swaying in light.
This must be what dark is for.

FLORESCENT SUN, CLOCK FOR A HEART

They'll never know,
These children of the future

Our same silence again,
The light when their leaf passes away,

Small flowers between my fingers stay,
While the luminescent moon becomes

A dial on their wrists,
Closing the hand with automation,

The birds at dawn are orchestrated now,
And fish swim according to size,

Do you not see the snow moving upward,
When it flies too close to earth,

They're on top of it all, the children of the future,
They grew up beyond a time when there were places of quiet,

Where the bees had hives of their own design, so
Let's go for a walk, just us,

Down the hill toward the park,
We'll watch the brook, hidden, moving on its own,

Then will come home, the two of us, before dark,
We'll know time by looking at the sky, one last time.

Before blue and grey calibrate to dusk.

THE HUNK

From under the truck
With a slight kiss of grease
Slides out her dream man
Blue eyes, black hair
Standing up sweet and tall
He's grabbing a smoke now
Lifting tan arms
Stretching his pecs
He pulls off his shirt
Lets it fall to the ground

This could be she thinks
The end of oceans of sadness —
But no, too quickly
His handprints are on her

The god of power and strength
Taut and lean could have
In another time be seen
As typical, desirable
Now no virtue can be won
What is done is done
He says, "Hey wait. No.
This is not who I am."

But he is what he is
Unless she wishes it, by mouth
Or breast or hand
How can she not
Blame the penis for the man.

COME TO A WEDDING
> *Same sex marriage legalized June 26, 2015*

It's remarkably astonishing
to be with each other
if you try – try to be
unassailable
not successful
that's what others think of you
know what you are / were/ could be
They will now make wedding cakes
and not turn you away
laugh at yourself
across the room and yes they changed
because it was meaningful (not useful)
when I don't want anything   I get something
now I want you – all of you
to celebrate
They're making wedding rings
and not turning you away
nothing may be all right for others
but for us nothing
but the best will do
It used to be bad
bad as a dollar which costs five
I know some things about them
(but just what they are I do not know)
so let them go
and on sheerest ground
warm as flowers opening on
earth sad and real as young girls
once growing old with books unopened
and letters left unread   now we can
go on
come on down
up   to the future

guess what word I can say
you
Oh unconquerable beauties
talking to the air
indenture yourself
come to the wedding

come to our wedding

PROPHECY

Too late I found what's truly mine.
This time, a pile of papers,

poems, on huge scraps, meant
to be nailed to his cut boards

how long had they been there
piled by the shed,

next to planks of polished wood.
The artist cut his shapes just right,

to mount my poems to stay, he'd said,
to be made permanent, he'd said.

That's why he left it all
for me to find one sunless day.

And where do I go for help?
Too soon , I saw they just didn't fit,

my poems upon his careful work.
At whose house can I seek help,

to press my paper into shapes, rounded
to nailed surfaces I did not make.

I followed the curve of his grain
as I should, with hand and glue,

refining the words to fit his frames.
Not out of vanity but sheer will of force,

trying the stain again and again,
smoothing the words to wrap around

what wood already stood.
What did it take to hear my own news,

that to insist is not to win.
That intention is not prophecy, that

I'd have to find my own wood
its own shape, my own shed.

I'm to cut my own planks, fit my own words,
make it new, not rely on the dead.

MAKING MEANING

Art is a full moon on the
branches of a broken country

and if you don't hold onto your own memories
don't ask anyone else to.

We can do anything to make art.
Call it vanity or transparency,

A wound, an enigma in the
soul, perhaps as practical as water

and just as useful.

Why debate the struggle of blossom
and field. I don't know what

we call struggle but it
spirals down, doesn't it,

slamming vision into waters.
I didn't know what was supposed to be pretty

and what was not.
At the same time, I was once

calm with love and its
torment – its sun – the

widening pool,
the humming of it. Listen I've known
cold flowers and nights

when I read alone in the dark.
There's no shame in

wanting unless it's having
without heart, and not knowing.

Then I saw what light made human.
 The man, The leaf.

EROS

*Plato's Symposium (380 B.C.) is the first written discussion
of Eros in human history.*

Believe it or not it started from a drinking spree
with six Greek notables, including Socrates,
so hungover from the night before
they decided to trade drinking for talk
instead of imbibing more.
What should be the topic?
How about the Greek god EROS.
They'd each take a turn with a theory.
– Just imagine this, now, as a movie
with six men in togas lying on couches –
Aristophanes said that it all began
when the first humans were embodied
in a huge wheel with breasts and penises,
and all the right body parts,
and then when sliced up, it was one big gamble:
some came out men loving women,
others, women toward women,
The rest, men turning to men.
What slice you got, was what you got.
Sounds weird, but another physician, said,
'Is Love not merely the filling up and emptying out of the body?'
This is where the first notions were born,
Love as the medium for ecstasy or vice,
according to what each province ruled lawful.
All agreed Love is otherworldly, something
we call in and carry our whole lives.
Yet, is it the source of beauty and happiness?
Or just a sexual union that summons the need
to bring us back for more, using envy and jealousy
at its core? What is this thing called "Love?"

One by one the important men argued a cosmic force
each speaking about himself, of course, as we do
when making our philosophic maunderings.
What they knew of Love was argued until the sweet
edges of dawn began sliding into light. They pondered:
Do we take from it forever? What do we keep?
And what do we throw away?
And then they turned from higher vision to a closer sight,
All were in agreement to formalize man-boy-love,
To our horror today
This, Eros, if ceremonial, state-approved, as proper and right.

*BILL BAILEY, WON'T YOU PLEASE COME HOME
Bill Bailey: Early American folk song

October with its dry leaves left at the picnic.
Another sympathy card
and what does it mean
if someone remembers your name in California?
Just a wasp stumbling into my light and

As to complaints about other men:
if I kissed two necks when you leaned down,
it's just because I didn't know any better.

You were never the jealous type anyway.
Camus says the only question is whether we live or die.
What answer is stolen from your silence?

That love is doomed as soon as petals are fallen?
That we overcome who we are by going away?
It doesn't mean you're not still a creature inside me

without tears and regret, once again leaving it all to me.

DEAR WORD PRISONER

From here you can see the water past craggy purple
rocks, stretches of green, rusted roof tops,
limned fields – yet this is not enough –
Spirits need language and what does it matter
unless we can describe the outdoor air at dark,
the late-night owl or fox,
walls leaning thick with loss,
stones large with dirt and leaves and moss—
Many souls lived and walked here on their way to heaven.
What led them on, glittering with love or luck?
Tell me what world we can speak of if it is not this,
the roaring of the ocean,
the emptiness of winter's gate –
I've visited these places but left
for all the words that could not touch them.
Anything I say! Squeal, cry, yelp, sigh out loud,
say something, mouth, say Summer,
talk of hands that held here. Whose?
The convert feathers rest silent in the tree
for lack of sound from heart.
Dear tongue, breath:
Don't leave me here alone with all this disappearing.

MUDRA

Every day I wake to find that I know nothing
The next day I find that I know even less
Today I learned that when I wake to consciousness
The cat will come to me
He doesn't need to see my open eyes
Today I learned the right hand on the
Heart will calm its beating
I will not know this until I touch my heart
After that again I will know nothing.

THIS POEM IS ASKING FOR YOUR LOVE

This poem is not usually like this
I don't know what came over it
It's mostly violet under the sun
with a large yellow parasol and a pond
with a center that never freezes
I swear I had no idea
I'm so used to trees of hearts and
cherries within its branches
I can't imagine
what woke this poem up
with a truth I never wanted
It called out the tower window and said
I was alone
That in itself is a morbid lie
I have long shadows in Autumn and clouds
anytime there is a sky
In fact everything was going so well until
this poem wanted to undress me
and bring back my love
and hold me close and rub
my forehead when I had a fever
It had no idea what trouble could come
from this so I wrote it
then I ran from it
now I can erase it
to show I never needed it after all
because don't you know, Poem,
if you have to *ask* for something
it's not a gift.

WHAT THE PSYCHIC SAID   65

"Did you know last life time you were a Mexican girl?
I see you sitting against a white wall with the sun barreling down
dazzling your shoulders. No trees anywhere.
You're staring out, as if from a vacuum, seeking, I don't know what.
Beside you, on the ground, a harness,
a thin horse in the distance eating pockets of grass.
No one can trespass here.
This is the landowner's yard.
The distance…the distance…I see a Mill. Can you
Remember? How thirsty you were?
Wood rotting, no water runs, but for a yellow stream.
How is it you were fluent? Perhaps by reading and writing
behind the barn with Big Papa?
Look at your dark eyes. No respite from the day ahead,
but for now you sit against the wall, hot with noontime.
Perhaps you're thinking of the Orient, a book you've read over
and over. The pictures. Oh the pictures.
Your eyes, wide, you wipe your face with our skirt.
Don't you realize that you came from labor? The fields?
Now you know why – this lifetime – why you cannot rest –
How you search for beauty? Why you can't stop dreaming of China."

I KISSED ROD JELLEMA
         (R.J. Amer, poet 1927-2018)

 It started in the '70s when
he left his bathrobe in my
bathroom by mistake
nothing wrong
Just a friendly gesture and so
in my dream
I kissed him on the mouth
It wasn't from Tinder, and there were
no trumpets blaring, and the floor
didn't cave in— no transgressions
just a sweet kiss
for one we love that we will see no longer
please note there was no jealous husband
with a stiletto waiting to surprise us
nor a tubular dying wife as a sentinel
peeking like a swordfish through the parted curtains
nothing like that, not even
a trail of stardust or a celestial moon above
It's just that I leaned upward
and kissed his bottom lip
just that, and nothing more.

JUST THIS AGAIN
The Buddha

From the palest soil
After the cold night
Within the shape of day
The edge of paradise
Flaming Winter's hill
Moving with the morning
Earthly beauty
Ready for eternity

If we walk a journey
Where will it lead
Or is the path the path
Where there is no harm
Merely the comfort
Of leaning in
Surrendering

RESURRECTION

You said if I came back a singer   you'd back me up on the sax   gardenia in my hair
you said the voiceless would be given sound and we'd be   out of the ordinary   unlimited space
birds eye view   out of the 3rd dimension   ring of truth   more broadly   a common cause
nothing to be hidden no more shame   to sing the truth   the iconography   the visceral   call
it a challenge   you said   insight   you said   would   change to story   that was the contour
for us   the intention   to tell all we knew   finally   in the church of forgiveness   in front
of an audience   I suspect   we can't   I said   I regret   we can't   prove it
he said   "What kind of person are you"   we'll be hiding behind music its strands of coherence no
let's not let's not come back   with the insight of past lives   let it rest in peace
expect things to happen   applause line   I love you   but let's stay dead   please   I pleaded.

HOLLOW

I fell for a guy who was going to die –
I knew at the moment I met him –
He was dying I tell you before he was born,
drifting to dark out of light, even I couldn't stop him.
Can you imagine holding candles in the hollow of your hand?
Can you imagine the wind blowing candles
held tight in the palm of your hand?
Do you see I've enclosed my heart in my hand?
While I bathed in the light coming out of the dark?
The deeper I got
the higher he climbed.
The moment I met him I knew
this is a guy who was born to die,
standing alone on a peak surrounded by sky.
The crickets were dying every day by his side.
The wish to be with the green as he fell to the trees –
I did it anyway.
I stood as long as I could
on the peak waiting. I stood as long as I could
until the crickets stopped singing.

KISS THE BRIDE

Don't look out the back window.
I've lived in the heartland
Of enchantment   so long
The top of my head open with a
Strong stream of sun struggling from the clouds
Sleeping by the brook
We cannot escape such edges   even if
I dreamed you up
The wind blows the blinds
The things once love   embodied
On the staircase
The ghost in the door   exotic
The tears on the pillow   spiritual
You have to dance
To the music you know   all
In equal measure   such a capacity
For potential kindness
What's funny about that
What alchemy do I qualify for
Let's have a baby
Start all over again   Let's be a family
How can they play at love in the movies like that
Tell me what to do.

VOYAGES
>	*for Cindy Maxted*

This poem never went to Africa
to sleep on the floor of the tent
or to treat children with scurvy.
This poem didn't even get as far as
Mexico where it could nestle
under the white hot sun in the warm
brown sand.
In fact, this poem's never been
anywhere at all and has led
a rather sheltered life,
but then again *Daring comes
from within* as a famous poet
once said,
and like the red flower blooming
on an otherwise greet prickly stalk
flames up to the top,
radiant, and brilliant, as one who dares
to give away the precious pebbles of her life
and someone else who dares to take them.

LET'S NOT SHOOT THE POETS

they fish at night
and dig by day
they were not born for death
their heavens are low enough to touch
flashing illumination and desire

they make Spring beautiful
They listen in their heads
for Autumn's breaking
they create and work
turning deadwood to life

society's not enough
so they fly above
its deception and
crash into clouds of meaning

the bucolic would not
exist but for their masterpiece

hostile fire, stay
away from the crush
of boats crowding
the shore – filled
with possible poets –

They are like animals
birthing but never forgetting
their loss   Poems
may be crushed but memory
is the hot gold made every day
They stay

HELP ME HERE

What is the poem that will finish my life?
A woman who loves her work goes
yes it is true from kiss to kiss yet

I'm just coming in from the moon,
That's why words change my reality
They sway—they turn—

They wind up in Heaven—
That's how the mind works,
And look at all the dead people here.

How can I manage them?
Maybe they can wait where the sky meets the sea
And one day (one by one) have a drink with me.

I don't know how else I can handle it.
Beyond time, so many of them,
The accumulations of the dead,

Each in a pale gray suit—
Those we had the best with—
Waiting in the great unknown to share again—

Even if happily addicted to their oyster colored sky.
Do they hear my words waiting for me?
It's too early in the poem to say.

FLYAWAY

For Joyce Varney Thompson (1922-2018)

Joyce was writing
every day from her 96-year bed
and her new novel would be
about life in Wales 100 years ago,
how she, a coal miner's daughter
worked in the "big house" as a kitchen helper.

Another book by the famed
salty-tongued, hot-tempered writer.

Once she told our Dean, who
wanted us to take more writing students
"...well, we can always put brooms up our asses
And sweep while we're doing it..."
That was 40 years ago before the fluorescent world of computers.

A gazelle, leaping from the mines, and I, her loyal follower,
will make this her best book
before her tenth decade
with my daily prompts and her fumbling emails
shattering the past to pick up pieces.

Tell me, Joyce, about how you got on the train
Help get the girl on the train, now,
how you got to the big house
you, all packed, wearing your woolen knickers
tell me about the train ride, Joyce.

"Well it was full of soldiers and smoke,
I stood up in the corner, two
girls kissing the soldiers,
gray brown coats,
crowded, smoking. I was afraid.
only fourteen..."

Write it like you said it, Joyce
But with all the story changes that she made,
she could not get on the train.

Two weeks ago she died in secrecy, days after she told me a dirty joke,
about a man caught naked with a woman when the husband arrived
and he ran out into the street and joined a marathon to get away
and the runner next to him asked if he always ran naked
and he said yes
and then the runner next to him asked
if he always wore a condom when he ran
and he said, 'only when it rains.'

When you put on the woolen knickers and you asked your Gran
why they itched "down there" and you asked what it was called
"down there" and she growled IT HAS NO NAME, Then she took
                    you to the train.

Flyaway   Joyce   to our future.
you were a mix of DylanThomas and Benny Hill.

                                        Flyaway
And of your 106-year-old roommate crying in Florida's blackout last year,
you said "Ha. You should have seen in the Blitz."

When Iphigenia was killed by Agamemnon, a doe
was found bleeding in her place.
What's here in your place, bleeding on the ground now—
but books, a man in the rain, a lush voice that spills,
eyes like saucers, coal smears.
And when you wrote of love there was so much pain it felt like happiness.

POPPIES IN THE SKY
For Prince

It could have been the blossoming, the tincture,
the perfume—
Perhaps it was a special poppy—
but he was told, if he picked it from the field,
he'd go right to heaven. And if he sniffed it twice
he'd turn into an angel.
I don't know what foolish friend led him to
that meadow—
I heard the stranger rode a pure white horse
and appeared as if from space.
We only know he took Prince to the dreaming waters,
and stayed with him, a long time, just to watch him pray.
Then the yoke from the Prancer was put around Prince.
It's said that Prince felt nothing on his neck, surrounded
as he was by such fragrance that he would
follow it willingly into his eternal sky.

THE PRINCE AND THE PAUPER

Did you see his red Corvette
parked at the top of the hill—
He was trying to get home,
the inquiry said,
Who could enter that marsh, so flooded,
He was last seen in regalia,
gold braid in the sun.
"Oh, he was a handsome lad,"
his neighbors whispered, "a shy one,
but, oh, inside his home, what sounds he'd make,
such a pleasing boy, such taste in clothes."
The crows flew overhead pounding the air,
"He died of Aids, you know."
The ravens argued "suicide, suicide, suicide."
"What does it matter?" the doves cried, "now
Prince will never be Prom King."
So what if his toothless uncle inherits,
money, the reporter tweeted,
he can only chew tea instead of steak.
"It was never that," his friends said, "never the money.
It was the sounds he'd make inside the house,
He'd bring out at night, finally safe in the spotlight."
Now that it's Autumn, and the rain has stopped,
do you see the bottom land
covered with purple mist, rich with greenery,
filled with birdsong of every kind—
He must have made it through.

IN PRAISE OF THE OASIS

The state of the car
the state of the car in disrepair
the sound I heard in the tire
the tire that was in disrepair
the sound I heard was a swing to the left
the left swing suddenly a ditch
from smooth sand on the right
from smooth sand to a rocky rut
I'm talking about swinging from a desert road
to a greenless rocky rut
the sweat in my eyes as I stumbled out
the sun and the flies on my eyes
the heat in my eyes and the flies
gleefully following me
I brush them from my eyes to
let me get to that old restaurant
I see in the distance, that one
with slated boards
faded red from the sunrise
faded blue from the sky
I hear all the way from there
an old record playing our song
in all this barrenness, the only song left
in a restaurant in a desert with the sun burning
a song that said you love me
in this barren waste
I can list the steps to get there
to the jukebox in the desert
A miracle
Its battered boards waving with the music.

LETTER FROM PUERTO RICO

If patience were a ray or sweet word
    It would never fail here
The keen bone of quiet is like faith
    Listen to the heat
    Feel the violet view
Cold motion has no reward
For Winter's just a painting on the wall
And Spring's wind is always perpendicular
    To time
Even if Lucille got the job you wanted
On the 5th floor with the Big Four
Shaking hands in her yellow suit
And chic bobbed hair
    She's dead now with unnarrowing
    Limits of grass
And the song succeeds with blackbirds
    And promise
Outlasting music's endnote.

THE LADY READS MY PALM

It's not luck you need to read the stars. It's the
shape of sorrow in your cup.
You once saw the wild ground
turn to shells beneath your feet.
You saw the gorgeous salt of the ocean
turning blue. You walked on melting sand and
now the lonely fervor quiets.
Take your marriage off the shelf. Dust it.
Make sense of this love where rock becomes air.
Who will sit with you.
Who will read your poems.
Please take back your ring
It's worth more than paper, gold or cash.
There's a song inside your finger
Saying more than a letter.
Take love.
Hold it to your ear and you will see
a vision
The shepherd moves across the fields.
You'll hear a name calling you home.

MAY DAY

He said they gave him
a white "Flash" suit—
like outer space wear.
They said, "put it on and
get into your cockpit."

What peril this was
he did not know
until they praised his plane
that held "your atom bomb."

A trail of thoughts
across his mind—
a sweep of stars beyond—
his children—their children.
his house—their house.

Pale with sadness
and hate, he knew what
he would do.

Ditch the plane in water!
the deepest part—
the bomb would dwell inert
and he would raft home from
the Turkish seas.

He was a calm man,
a survival expert—
he figured it out—
maybe four months.

His heart was a meteor
exploding in his children's
backyard under the apple tree—

It dazzled the swing set,
the rowboat filled
with toys and sand—
his wife in a pink and white
sundress
looking up at the sky.

REFUGEES

At sunset
they do not fold their
tents like tourists in Aruba.

How shall we dress our children
for their first fine day at school—
The refuged do not worry about
a dress, a suit a fine day
at school.

And look at the photos
of the African child dying in the camp
with flies on his eyelids.
He has no wish for the teddy bear
sent from UNICEF.

Did you read about that child
in Arizona
beaten to death
for soiling his pants?

Did you see that mother
outside the post office
hurl her one-year-old by his arm
into her SUV?

So you dreamed last night about a baby
that you forgot to feed.
It's not a dream the refugees
can afford to dream.

This is why you write a poem.
In fact, It's all that you can do.
You cannot know more, unless

you are that child with a broken arm,
or, the Mother with
a baby crying at her drying breasts.

If you are not with the exiled,
captured, stripped and sold, then
you are the one who must write this poem.

THE TRIBE

of soaring strangers, the curious, the blooming—
Joseph Brodsky in a Labor Camp for writing the people's language,
Adrienne Rich ... "Take ourselves more seriously/
...a deeper listening cleansed of oratory, formulas..."
I thank them for the future—
The double narratives of Louise Gluck, spacious and small for
Memory not yet imagined of children separated at the border.
The real   the will   Rita's "Thomas and Beulah" bringing to life
More than a muse could create.
You ask about resistance and how we can keep going, I say,
Blake's revolutionary "Meet on the coast/ glowing with blood ..."
Words rinsed off from a corrupt court   Patricia Smith: "All my fists at once?"
Espada with "Music and Spanish rose before the bread .../Praise and bread..."
We praise the bread of those who are our tribe and where we are strong,
Where we belong. Alexie, "Everyone is a half-breed ..." even those on either side
Of the fence   where   language flies across   like unchained birds.

WHITE

Remember how we tried to help, no sense of the difficulty,
eschewing advice, I took your white paint, outback,
and tried to fill in, the worn parts of the doors,
the cracks in our walls.
How did I know it would drip and drizzle,
down the doorknobs, although I slapped and stalled the brush.
Why didn't I realize the thickness
the mix, how it splatters on glass, separates, like
white blood everywhere, even on squirrels running by,
carrying it, turning all the trees in the forest white.
How kind you were to come out, without reproach,
to remove the entire back of the house, so easily.
It was getting dark, and there you were,
in your white shirt with tiny blue flowers,
holding a large box of flowers for me.
You fixed it all, with a twist of your wrist,
planning to replace it with fresh wood, saving it for our future.
Although no time to paint it right now,
but always a chance for tomorrow. Trees sparking white with snow,
Who could have known beneath them,
you would be a dead soldier, in a box of dust,
next to the raw lumber of our construction.

ATHENA'S DIRTY LITTLE SECRET

"I've brought an army of angels
to bring the settlers home safe
I've battled all love that was not of use
I turned a cobbled walk into a stream of gold
I've worn a white flash suit to prevent
explosions on earth
I've taken the moon and held it like desire hot in my hand
I've posed as your confident so that I could keep you safe
All these things to make happiness my journey of strength
All these things to guarantee I did not disappoint
the gods as A Woman
And as A Woman I proved that an abyss is
merely from looking down at jagged rocks yet
from that place I opened the windows of clouds from a high tower
and saw   caught as I am in midair   as the goddess of power
that the green stands still on earth   the geese are clucking
I saw the empty shoes from children left beside the stair
I saw them coming up the hill toward me
I saw that this is what I wanted all along
to pour milk   to open the door   I wanted to be there."

WHAT CAN I SAY TO MAKE YOU HAPPY

If I were to compose
from the cloth
of your grieving
how would I breathe light from fabric

the machine casts a shadow
that still lives
it fills the air with satin
not shallow wool
silk that moves
like sand in wind.

If I could say one word
that would not constrict
what would it be

the metal pumps its movement
so skirt and shirt and
dress are kin to skin

what do I have to do
with the making of anything

but say that good words have no age
and will wrap their own way to you
from any loving seamstress.

JUST THIS
  The Buddha
  for Phyllis Culham and Bob Ertman

The water to the left turning
then to the right past barbed fences
leaning past trees once again alive
up then down the valley you like
what you see spring summer
it doesn't matter to walk by the water
is to see white seasons turning green to blue
swarms of flying sparks with wings in the
closing darkness then morning comes
past your sight verging so we want to close
our eyes then to open to find some meaning
find purpose for movement and we slow down
then we find there is no meaning but motion.
Just this. Again. Just this.

ATHENA SEES

the sleeping sun slipping away
as if it had another day
yet how good and true the light is
how it never lets us down
showing up again and again
from its sunny dream
every single day from every single night
like a basket of happiness
fair to everyone, rich and poor alike,
and how much, how much you can love
the sky because it will always be there.

WEATHER REPORT

These white stripes of day achieve
more than we could possibly hope for, with
curtains –thin movements – shielding the
curious birds.
Pure pleasure is illuminated by each
sequence of bright and shadow on the wall.
Think of this –
Light stands for nothing but itself!
Who can say that—
I read in today's paper a woman got seven
Years for killing someone by accident.

Now a flat formation of rain in the distance
threatens to slash our virtue.
Nothing is hopeless here in Rincon:
hills, palms, yellow, blue, green,
filtered through fern.
I can leave this room with its sensations and silhouettes.
I can walk the yard through the gate to enter my own devotions.

AT THE NAVAL ACADEMY POOL

Underwater light twigs on first year minions and
midshipmen swimming with masks
frog feet turning churning new boys' new hair young you over there
which of you will surface in the water when the deck is hit
and who among you will serve the other or go under in confusion
who will try and which one will surface and
who dives in the unwanted dark more than once
will Parkinson's ripen in the one who would be a Seal
whose child will run away from you destined swimmer
will you reach 80 and have a cane
which of you will have your finger on the weapon
who will say your name in rhetoric 100 years from now
what wife will attract you and which one will leave you
these are the velvet days take your mark swimmers.

About the Author

Grace Cavalieri is Maryland's tenth Poet Laureate.

She's the author of 26 books and chapbooks of poetry and 20 short-form and full-length plays. Among other honors Grace holds The Associated Writing Program's George Garrett Award, plus the Pen-Fiction, the Allen Ginsberg, Bordighera Poetry, and Paterson Poetry awards; the "Annie" Award; The inaugural Folger Shakespeare Library Columbia Award; The National Award from The Commission On Working Women; and The CPB Silver Medal. Her latest book was *Showboat* (Goss183, 2019) about 25 years as a Navy wife. Her latest play "Quilting The Sun" was produced at the Theater for the New City, NYC in 2019.

She founded and produces "The Poet and the Poem" for public radio, now from the Library of Congress, celebrating 43 years on-air.